CHRISTMAS
PLANNER

CW00607175

FAMILY MATTERS ✓

CHRISTMAS PLANNER

HELEN DOUGLAS-COOPER

WARD LOCK

A WARD LOCK BOOK

First published in the UK 1991
by Ward Lock
(a Cassell imprint)
Villiers House
41/47 Strand
London
WC2N 5JE

Distributed in the United States
by Sterling Publishing Co., Inc.
387 Park Avenue South, New York, NY 10016–8810

Distributed in Australia
by Capricorn Link (Australia) Pty Ltd
P.O. Box 665, Lane Cove, NSW 2066

British Library Cataloguing in Publication Data
Douglas-Cooper, Helen
    Christmas Planner. –(Family Matters).
    1. Christmas activities
    I. Title   II. Series
    790.1

    ISBN 0–7063–6949–1

Typeset in 11 on 11½ point ITC Garamond Light by
Columns Design and Production Services Ltd, Reading

Printed and bound in Great Britain by
William Collins & Sons, Glasgow

CONTENTS

INTRODUCTION

When the summer holidays are over and thoughts start to turn to Christmas, people tend to have mixed feelings. Inspiration, enthusiasm and ideas for new things to try are tempered by memories of all the work and effort involved in the preparations. Resolutions about making all the decorations for the house or giving a sit-down dinner for twenty on Christmas Eve fade as the time draws closer. Yet everybody wants to create a lovely Christmas for their family each year.

The answer is to start early. Plan everything well ahead. Draw up a basic shopping checklist and do as much as possible of the shopping and cooking in advance. Make a timetable that covers all the other routine household tasks as well as the preparations. Prepare as much of the Christmas dinner as possible before the big day, together with a plan of action so that you can glide calmly through Christmas morning confident that nothing has been forgotten.

Don't think that you need to do everything yourself – sharing the preparations is part of the build-up, and it makes it more fun and less hard work. If you are short of volunteers in the family, delegate some of the tasks. Or make a list of things to be made or done, and ask everyone to choose one or two things from it.

Around Christmas, arrangements often change at the last minute due to bad weather, illness or eleventh-hour invitations. Don't be thrown by this. Again, if things are well planned and you feel on top of it all, this should not be a problem.

The majority of us need to make lists of the things we must remember to get or do, although endless lists begin to be ignored and will probably get lost anyway. However, it is worth making lists – with deadlines – of the most important things to be done. If you make a list, do try to keep to it, otherwise it becomes a depressing reminder of what you have not done instead of being an aid to getting things done.

To help you organize and achieve a smooth-running Christmas that you are able to enjoy as much as everyone else, this book is full of checklists, ideas and information. It has suggestions for menus, cooking, presents, entertaining. It has ideas for decorating the house. It contains checklists for shopping, household chores and entertaining. Take what is relevant for your Christmas and fill in the master plan at the end in order to help you remember everything that needs to be done, and by when. The separate timetable for cooking Christmas dinner should ensure that you have as much time and energy for enjoying Christmas Day (well – almost) as the rest of the family.

Chapter 1

EARLY DECISIONS

As early as possible in the autumn, you should start discussing plans for Christmas.

What type of Christmas will you have? Will it be traditional or do you want to do something different? Do you want to have lots of people around, or do you want to have a quiet Christmas with just your close family?

What entertaining do you want to do? Will you have house guests? If so, for how long? Will you give a party over the Christmas holiday? If so, what kind – a buffet, a drinks party, a party for the children?

What about the cooking? How many will you be feeding for Christmas dinner – how many do you feel you can cope with? Are you going to make the pudding, the cake, mincemeat and so on yourself?

What other things do you want to make yourself – decorations, presents – or what special things do you want to do? It is nice to create family traditions that become part of Christmas every year.

And what other events might be taking place, that need to be taken into account in the planning?

Having made these decisions you can begin drawing up a plan of action, especially for those things that you want to get on with early: shopping for presents, beginning the advance cooking, sending out invitations.

It is also worth checking now on last posting dates, if you need to send parcels abroad. Don't forget, too, that a package or card sent early by sea will cost you less than one sent later by air.

BUDGETING

Christmas can be a very expensive time of year, and although no one wants to deny their family a good time, most of us want to keep some control over the amount that we spend – the cost of Christmas seems to run away as it draws closer. The best way to keep on top of the cost is to decide on your plans and then draw up a budget. It can be quite simple, and can be broken up under headings:

☆ Food
☆ Presents
☆ Postage
☆ Cards and wrapping

☆ Donations
☆ Tree
☆ Pantomimes etc.
☆ Travelling

WAYS OF MAKING YOUR MONEY GO FURTHER

☆ Make the cake, pudding, mincemeat etc. This is much cheaper than buying them ready-made.
☆ Money can be saved by making presents. Home-made food items such as chutneys, bottled fruit, cakes, biscuits and sweets, little knitted or embroidered gifts, are always popular and seem extra-special for being hand-made.
☆ Decorations can also be made much more cheaply than buying them.
☆ Start shopping early and spread the spending over two to three months, a little at a time.
☆ Each time you go out shopping, buy a couple of items towards Christmas.

Chapter 2

CHRISTMAS FOOD AND SHOPPING

Having decided on what you are doing for Christmas, the number of people you will have on Christmas Day, whether you are giving a party etc., the first job is to plan the cooking that will need to be done.

Make a list of all the dishes that you will need for the main Christmas meals, the cake, seasonal extras, and plan the menus for the other meals, plus parties.

Take into account special diets of anyone in the family or among your guests, such as vegetarians, vegans, or requirements of very young or elderly members of the family. Then work out how they can most easily be accommodated within the planned menus. If you do have to cater for a special diet, try to plan some meals that everyone can eat, unless they are very restrictive, as this will cut down on the work.

THREE MONTHS TO FOUR WEEKS BEFORE CHRISTMAS

Having decided on what you are going to cook, you can draw up a plan of what to do in advance and when. Allocate two or three days or half days to Christmas cooking. Also, make sure that you have got all the recipes you need; if you want to try a new version of Christmas pudding, for example, now is the time to look around for one.

It is worth stocking up the freezer with some basic supplies specially for Christmas, as a well-stocked freezer will enable you to cater for family meals, unexpected guests and entertaining. You can also do some advance preparation for Christmas dinner, such as stuffings, sauces and brandy butter, and store them in the freezer. Remember to defrost and clean out the freezer before you begin stocking it for Christmas.

Batches of stock – light and dark – are essential for gravies and sauces and for making quick vegetable soups. Soups can be made in advance, reduced rapidly and frozen in ice trays. Basic stews can be frozen, and can have some extra vegetables added when served. Extra puddings, fruit pies, ice creams and sorbets can be frozen; pancakes are useful to have in the freezer, and can be used either for a savoury dish or for a pudding. If you like to have one or two alternatives to the Christmas cake, these too can be made and frozen. If you are cooking for a vegetarian, soaked and cooked beans and pulses can be frozen. Pastry and pizza dough are always useful items to have in store. Items such as these will not be wasted if they are not in the end needed over Christmas.

One good way to organize the cooking is to batch together different types of dishes. For example, you could spend an afternoon on pastry-making, another on making stock and soups, another on desserts, and so on. And if you put all the Christmas cooking together in one tray or basket in the freezer you will save time when you come to need them.

Now is the time to check your cooking equipment and appliances. Before you launch into any major cooking sessions, check that you have the correct-sized cake tins, a roasting tin large enough to take the turkey, plenty of mince pie tins, enough freezer containers for what you are cooking, and any other equipment that you might need. If any of your household appliances are due for a service, have it done now.

- house decorations
- invitations
- nuts
- stamps
- tree (buy late, as with holly and mistletoe)

- tree decorations
- tree lights and spare bulbs
- wrapping paper, ribbon and tags

TALKING TURKEY

Turkeys can be bought fresh, either ordered in advance from the butcher or bought at the last minute from the supermarket; or they can be bought frozen, again either in advance or at the last minute. However, turkeys are best fresh. If you order one from the butcher well in advance – about four weeks before Christmas – you know that the matter is taken care of. At the same time you can order any other meats, such as ham, goose or a joint of beef or pork, that you might need over the holiday. You can then collect your order a day or two before Christmas.

WHAT TO ASK FOR

Fresh birds are usually sold oven-ready – plucked and drawn, and the weight specified includes the head and giblets. Sometimes birds are sold complete, which means that they are clean plucked but still have their head and feet as well as the giblets.

If you are buying a frozen turkey, try and find one that is either fresh-style or free-range, as these are frozen without extra water.

WHAT SIZE TURKEY?

For a fresh, oven-ready turkey allow:

☆ 350–450 g/12 oz–1 lb per person for a bird up to 7.5 kg/16 lb
☆ 450–550 kg/1–1¼ lb per person for a bird over 7.5 kg/16 lb

A very large bird – 10.5–11.5 kg/23–25 lb – will give sixteen to twenty generous portions. If the bird is complete (or clean-plucked) allow 1.5 kg/3 lb for the head, feet and giblets before calculating the size you need. Therefore, for the average-size family you will need a bird that is 6 kg/12–15 lb oven-ready weight (equivalent to 7 kg/14–16 lb complete).

For a frozen turkey:

A frozen bird loses about 5 per cent of its weight on defrosting, so calculate the size you need as for a fresh oven-ready turkey, and add on 5 per cent.

Read any instructions on the wrapping, and get it into your own freezer as quickly as possible so that it has no chance to begin thawing.

THE LAST TWO WEEKS

This is when the panic really starts to set in. However, if you organized yourself well ahead, and have followed the plan you set out earlier, you should now have the cake and pudding safely made and maturing nicely, all manner of basic supplies stocked in the cupboard, a variety of pastries, sauces, stocks, cakes, desserts and other useful items tucked away in the freezer, and the turkey and other meats on order from the butcher.

If you have got behind with the preparations, or if you are only just beginning to think about Christmas, do not go mad and try to do everything yourself at this stage. Make use of the wide range of high-quality, ready-made goods sold in the supermarkets. Some even sell ready-stuffed, frozen turkeys.

MARZIPAN (ALMOND PASTE) THE CAKE

This needs to be done about seven days before Christmas, but can be done ten to fourteen days in advance if you are ahead with the preparations.

THE TURKEY

Order the turkey if you have not done so already (see p. 12).

MAKE MINCE PIES

These can be made ahead of time, as they will keep for a few days in an airtight tin (see p. 40). It is useful anyway to have a batch made by now to offer visitors.

PREPARATIONS FOR CHRISTMAS DINNER

Finalize the menu, if you have not done so already.

If you want to have a first course, keep it light, such as a thin vegetable soup, potted shrimps or jellied tomato ring.

Decide what vegetables to have with the turkey; sprouts with chestnuts are traditional, but many different vegetables go well with it.

Decide on the other accompaniments: bacon rolls, chipolata sausages, bread sauce and chestnut sauce are all popular.

If you are catering for a vegetarian, choose a simple dish that goes well with the traditional accompaniments to a turkey, such as nut loaf or rissoles, or a vegetable soufflé.

Decide whether you want to serve an alternative to Christmas pudding.

Decide which cheeses to serve: Stilton is the traditional cheese to serve at Christmas, and you could also offer a hard cheese such as Cheshire or Lancashire and/or a mild, soft cheese.

Several items can be prepared, or part prepared, and stored in the freezer:

☆ Stuffings (see pp. 23–4)
☆ Brandy butter (see p. 32)
☆ Sprouts – peeled and blanched

CHILDREN IN THE KITCHEN

Children love to join in the preparations, and there are all kinds of things for them to do in the kitchen.

Very young children can help with stirring cool dishes, cutting out biscuits and scones with cutters, and decorating biscuits and cakes.

Five- to seven-year-olds can help with chopping up fruit and vegetables (with a blunt knife), rolling out dough and preparing cake tins.

Older than this, they can make simple items on their own, such as biscuits and sweets (see pp. 46–50), sponge cakes, mince pies, iced buns and dips.

Remember – when children are cooking, they should be supervised all the time.

THE LAST FEW DAYS

As Christmas draws close, the number of major cooking items should come down to a manageable quantity. The cake needs to be iced, although this can be done a week or so ahead if you have the time. If you have bought a frozen turkey, allow plenty of time for defrosting it (see below). If you prefer to make fresh stuffing for the turkey, rather than making it ahead and freezing it, do so a day or two ahead, as it will keep for this length of time in an airtight container in the fridge. This is also a good time to draw up the timetable for cooking Christmas dinner.

Stick menus and the Christmas dinner timetable in the kitchen where everyone can see them. It is then easy for helpers to stand in for you while you take a break or if you get held up by some chore or activity.

ICE AND DECORATE THE CAKE

If you want to give the cake two layers of icing, the first can be done up to a week ahead (see pp. 37–40).

DEFROST THE TURKEY

A frozen turkey needs plenty to time to defrost – several hours or even days, depending on its size (see p. 21). It will keep in the fridge for about twenty-four hours after thawing, so err on the side of allowing too much time.

If you are having a fresh turkey collect it, and remove the giblets as soon as you get home.

LAST-MINUTE SHOPPING

Refer to your basic shopping checklist in case you have overlooked anything, or if supplies are getting low already. In particular, items like icing sugar are liable to run out as icing for the cake uses up a lot, and suddenly there is not enough left for the brandy butter.

The following list covers fresh items that need to be left until the last minute, and of which you may need extra supplies over the Christmas holiday.

- bread
- butter and/or similar spreads
- cheeses, blue, hard and soft
- cream, fresh

- apples, eating and cooking
- bananas
- Brussels sprouts
- carrots
- cauliflower
- celery
- chestnuts
- grapefruit
- grapes
- lettuce

- eggs
- milk, including some UHT (and some can be frozen)
- yogurt

- lemons
- mushrooms
- onions
- oranges
- parsnips
- potatoes
- salad stuff
- tomatoes
- tangerines

CHRISTMAS DINNER

The best approach to preparing Christmas dinner is to make a detailed timetable that covers every aspect of cooking and dishing up the meal. It should also incorporate any other activities that you want to be involved in on Christmas morning. There are several jobs that can be done on Christmas Eve, which will make your own Christmas Day more enjoyable.

DRAWING UP A TIMETABLE

1. Decide at what time you want to sit down to eat, and work back from that.
2. The item that requires the longest time is the turkey, so start with that. Aim to have the turkey cooked 30 minutes before you want to start the meal, as it benefits from 'resting' for a while before being carved; this also gives you plenty of time to make gravy and dish

up the vegetables. Then work out the total cooking time according to the turkey's weight (see p. 22), and this will give you the time that the turkey should go into the oven. Working back again, allow 30 minutes for preparing and stuffing the turkey, at the same time pre-heating the oven; this will give you your starting time in the morning.

3. Go back to the time you want to eat, and work out at what time the pudding should go on; make a note of the time that the water should go on to pre-heat.

4. Work out at what time the potatoes should go in to roast; remember to include peeling them either early in the morning, or the day before.

5. Include any preparations and/or finishing off for the first course.

6. Include preparations and cooking for the accompanying vegetables according to the recipes you have chosen; if boiling green vegetables, make a note of the time that the water should go on for pre-heating.

7. Decide whether you want to serve an alternative to Christmas pudding, and which sauces to serve with the pudding. Brandy butter is the traditional accompaniment, but you could serve cream or hot custard – either home-made or powdered – if your family prefer.

In planning the timetable you also need to bear in mind how many items you can have on top of the cooker and in the oven at one time, and you should plan how to keep food hot once it is cooked.

ON CHRISTMAS EVE

- Make giblet stock (see p. 26)
- Make/defrost stuffings for turkey (see pp. 23–4). However, do not stuff the turkey in advance of cooking it
- Make/defrost brandy butter and other sauces for the pudding (see p. 32)
- Prepare first course, if having one

- Peel potatoes, and store completely covered in cold water, in a bowl in the fridge
- Prepare other vegetables
- Make/defrost breadcrumbs for the bread sauce.

BASIC TIMETABLE FOR CHRISTMAS MORNING

This timetable is based on an average-sized turkey of 6 kg (12–14 lb) oven-ready weight, and a lunch time of two o'clock. You will need to incorporate your choice of first course and accompanying vegetables.

7.30	Prepare and stuff turkey Pre-heat oven
7.50	Put fat in roasting tin in oven to melt
8.00	Put in turkey
10.30	Make brandy butter (if not done already) Peel potatoes (if not done already) Prepare other vegetables (if not done already)
11.45	Put on water to steam pudding Put fat in roasting tin in oven to melt, for potatoes
12.00	Put on pudding Put in potatoes to roast
1.00	Put plates and serving dishes to warm
1.15	Put on water for green vegetables Make bread sauce
1.30	Turkey cooked – transfer to serving dish and keep warm Dish up roast potatoes and keep warm Put on vegetables Dish up vegetables – retain cooking liquid for making gravy Make gravy

1.45   Make hot custard (if relevant)
        Turn out pudding
2.00   Serve Christmas dinner

Other jobs to be done/remind others to do:
- Lay the table
- Decorate the table
- Put out nibbles, sweets etc., in bowls
- Set coffee tray for the end of the meal
- Uncork/decant wine, port; put out other drinks and glasses

Chapter 3

CHRISTMAS RECIPES

TURKEY

DEFROSTING A FROZEN TURKEY

Remove the polythene wrapping and cover the bird with foil to prevent it drying out. Remove the giblets and neck as soon as possible. The table that follows gives you an idea of defrosting times for a small, medium and large turkey but you should follow the instructions on the wrapping.

Weight	Thawed at room temperature 18°C/65°F	Thawed in refrigerator 4°C/40°F
	Hours	Hours
2.5–3 kg/5–6 lb	18–20	40–50
4.5–5.5 kg/10–12 lb	26–29	66–70
9.5–11.5 kg/20–22 lb	35–40	82–86

PREPARING THE TURKEY

chestnut stuffing for the neck (p. 24)
sausagemeat stuffing for the body (p. 23)
5–6 fat bacon rashers
fat for basting
450 g/1 lb pork chipolatas
string for trussing

Pre-heat the oven to 220°C/425°F/gas 7. When heated, melt the fat in the roasting tin.

Wipe the bird inside and outside with a clean, damp cloth. Stuff the neck end with the chestnut stuffing, and the body cavity with sausagemeat stuffing.

To truss the bird, first lay it on its back. Pass the string under the bird and bring the ends up between the body and thigh on each side. Turn the bird over and loop the string through the elbow joint on each side. Wrap the flap of skin over the neck end and twist the points of the wings over the flap of skin to hold it in place. Pull the string firmly, but not so tight that it tears the skin, and tie in the centre to hold the wings in place. Take the string back to the drumsticks. Loop the string around the drumsticks and parson's nose, and tie off. Turn the bird on to its back.

Place the bird in the roasting tin and baste well. Lay the bacon rashers over the breast, cover the bird loosely with foil and put in the oven.

ROASTING TIMES FOR TURKEY

15–20 minutes at 220°C/425°F/gas 7; then reduce the oven to 180°C/350°F/gas 4 and cook, according to its weight, for example:

Weight	Hours
2.5–3 kg (5–6 lb)	3–3½
4.5–5.5 kg (10–12 lb)	4½–5
9.5–11 kg (20–25 lb)	6½–7½

Remember to pre-heat the oven to the required temperature. Baste the turkey regularly.

About 30 minutes before the end of the cooking time, separate the chipolatas and add them to the fat in the roasting tin. If they will not fit in, roast them in a separate tin.

About 20 minutes before the end of the cooking time, remove the foil and bacon strips to allow the breast to brown.

To test whether the bird is cooked, pierce the thick part of the thigh with a skewer. The juices should run clear, and show no sign of pinkness.

When the bird is cooked, remove the trussing string, place the turkey on a warmed serving dish and put it somewhere to keep warm.

FITTING THE TURKEY IN THE OVEN

A 6 kg (13 lb) turkey will fit into an oven with a capacity of 0.07 cu m (0.09 cu yd)/42 × 40 × 40 cm (16½ × 15¾ ×15¾ in).

If your oven is smaller, or the bird larger, it may be possible to fit the bird in by removing the legs and cooking them separately. When cooked, reassemble the bird using fine wooden skewers, and hide the join with a garnish such as watercress.

SAUSAGEMEAT STUFFING

liver of the turkey, washed and trimmed
1 kg/2¼ lb sausagemeat
100 g/4 oz soft white breadcrumbs
2 × 15 ml spoons/2 tbsp chopped parsley
2 × 15 ml spoons/2 tsp dried mixed herbs
1 × 2.5 ml spoon/½ tsp grated nutmeg
1 × 2.5 ml spoon/½ tsp ground mace
salt and pepper
2 eggs, beaten

Chop the liver finely and mix it with the sausagemeat and breadcrumbs. Add the herbs and spices and season to taste. Stir in the beaten egg to bind the mixture.

Use to stuff the tail end of a turkey.

MAKES ABOUT 1.25 KG/2½ LB (ENOUGH FOR A LARGE TURKEY).

CHESTNUT STUFFING

800 g/1¾ lb chestnuts in their shells or 550 g/1 ¼ lb shelled
or canned chestnuts
125–250 ml/4½–8 fl oz chicken stock or giblet stock
50 g/2 oz butter
1 large mild onion, chopped
salt and pepper
pinch of ground cinnamon
1 × 2.5 ml spoon/½ tsp granulated sugar

If using fresh chestnuts, make a slit in the rounded side of their shells and boil them for 20 minutes. Remove the shells and skins while hot.

Put the chestnuts in a pan with just enough stock to cover them. Heat to boiling point, then reduce the heat, cover and simmer until the chestnuts are tender. Drain, and reserve the stock. Rub the chestnuts through a fine wire sieve into a bowl.

Melt the butter in a small saucepan and fry the onion over moderate heat until translucent but not turning brown. Add to the chestnuts. Season to taste and stir in the cinnamon and sugar. Stir in just enough of the reserved stock to make a soft stuffing.

Use to stuff the neck or tail end of a turkey, and place another stuffing in the body.

MAKES ABOUT 800 G/1¾ LB (ENOUGH FOR A LARGE TURKEY).

BACON ROLLS

streaky bacon rashers, rinds removed
cocktail sticks

Cut each rasher in half crossways, roll up and secure with a cocktail stick. Place in the roasting tin around the turkey about half an hour before the end of the cooking time. When done, remove from the tin, remove the cocktail sticks and keep warm. Use to garnish the turkey.

BREAD SAUCE

450 ml/³/₄ pt milk
1 large onion, about 200 g/7 oz, chopped
3 cloves
blade of mace
6 peppercorns
2 allspice berries
2 bay leaves
75 g/3 oz dried white breadcrumbs
2 × 15 ml spoons/2 tbsp butter
salt and pepper
2 × 15 ml spoons/3 tbsp single cream (optional)

Heat the milk very slowly in a saucepan with the onion, spices and bay leaves. Cover the pan and infuse over a gentle heat for 30 minutes. Strain the liquid and return it to the pan.

Stir in the breadcrumbs and butter and season to taste. Heat to just below simmering point and maintain that temperature for 20 minutes. Stir in the cream, if used.

MAKES ABOUT 450 ML/³/₄ PT

CHESTNUT SAUCE

200 g/7 oz chestnuts in their shells
375 ml/13 fl oz chicken stock
pinch of ground cinnamon
small strip of lemon rind
25 g/1 oz butter
salt and pepper
5 × 15 ml spoons/5 tbsp single cream (optional)

Make a slit in the rounded side of the chestnut shells and boil them for 20 minutes. Remove the shells and skins while hot. Put the chestnuts in a saucepan with the stock, cinnamon and lemon rind. Heat to simmering point, and simmer gently for 30 minutes or until the chestnuts are very tender. Remove the lemon rind.

Rub the chestnuts and liquid through a sieve, or puree in a blender. Return the puree to the pan, add the butter, and season to taste. Heat gently for 2–3 minutes. Stir in the cream, if used, just before serving.

MAKES ABOUT 375 ML/13 FL OZ

GIBLET STOCK

1 set of giblets, washed and trimmed
2 onions, quartered
1 carrot, trimmed and quartered
1 celery stick, thickly sliced
2 bay leaves
6 peppercorns
salt (optional)
600 ml/1 pt water

Put all the ingredients into a saucepan and heat to boiling point. Cover the pan, reduce the heat and simmer gently for 1 hour.

Leave the stock to cool slightly. Then, using a large spoon, skim off the fat. Strain the stock, cool and chill until required.

MAKES ABOUT 500 ML/18 FL OZ

GRAVY

pan juices
2 × 15 ml spoons/2 tbsp plain flour
500 ml/18 fl oz giblet stock or water from cooking vegetables
6–8 × 15 ml spoons/6–8 tbsp red wine (optional)
2 × 15 ml spoons/2 tbsp redcurrant jelly
salt and pepper

After roasting the turkey, pour off most of the fat from the roasting tin, leaving about 5 × 15 ml spoons/5 tbsp of fat and sediment in the bottom of the tin. Sprinkle the flour into the pan juices and blend thoroughly. Put over a medium heat and cook until browned.

Take off the heat and add in about one third of the liquid, stirring thoroughly until smooth. Add the rest of the liquid and stir until blended. Put back on the heat and bring to the boil, stirring all the time. Boil for 3–4 minutes. Stir in the wine, if used, and the redcurrant jelly. Taste and season with salt and pepper if necessary.

Strain the gravy into a warmed gravy boat, and serve very hot.

MAKES ABOUT 600 ML/1 PT

ALTERNATIVES TO TURKEY

ROAST GOOSE WITH PRUNE STUFFING

1 large goose, with giblets
1 onion, quartered
1 litre/1¾ pt water
½ lemon
salt and pepper
350 g/12 oz prunes, soaked and drained
450 g/1 lb cooking apples, roughly chopped
1 × 15 ml spoon/1 tbsp flour
2 × 15 ml spoons/2 tbsp redcurrant jelly

Simmer the giblets and onion in the water until reduced by half. Strain, skim the fat from the top and set the stock aside.

Weigh the goose and calculate the cooking time at 20 minutes for every 450 g/1 lb. Pre-heat the oven to 230°C/450°F/gas 8.

Cut away any visible excess fat. Rinse the inside of the bird, rub the skin with lemon and season with salt and pepper. Prick all over the skin many times with a darning needle.

Stone and chop the prunes. Mix with the apple and season. Pack the fruit into the bird.

Place the goose on a trivet in a roasting tin, and put in the oven. Reduce the temperature immediately to 180°C/350°F/gas 4, and cook for the calculated time.

When the goose is cooked, remove it to a heated serving dish and drain the fat, retaining the juices in the pan. Off the heat, stir in the flour, then gradually pour in the reduced giblet stock. Put over the heat and bring to the boil. Stir in the redcurrant jelly. Season to taste.

Serve with apple sauce and onion forcemeat balls.

SERVES 6–8

APPLE SAUCE

450 g/1 lb cooking apples, sliced
2 × 15 ml spoons/2 tbsp water
15 g/½ oz butter or margarine
grated rind and juice of ½ lemon
granulated sugar

Put the apples into a saucepan with the water, butter or margarine and lemon rind. Cover and cook over a low heat until the apple is reduced to a pulp. Beat until smooth, and rub through a sieve or puree in a blender or food processor. Reheat the sauce with the lemon juice and sugar to taste.

MAKES ABOUT 375 ML/13 FL OZ

SAGE AND ONION FORCEMEAT

2 small onions, sliced
4 young sage leaves or 1 × 2.5 ml spoon/½ tsp dried sage
100 g/4 oz soft white breadcrumbs
50 g/2 oz butter or margarine
salt and pepper
1 egg, beaten

Put the onions into a saucepan with a little water and parboil. Drain the onions and chop them finely. Scald the fresh sage leaves, if used, and chop them finely. Mix the chosen sage together with the onions and breadcrumbs. Melt the butter, add to the stuffing and season to taste. Mix thoroughly.

Add enough beaten egg to bind the mixture and shape it into balls. Fry in deep or shallow fat until golden brown and cooked.

MAKES ABOUT 175 G/6 OZ

BAKED HAM

a whole raw ham joint (fore hock or gammon cuts such as gammon hock)
apricot jam
canned pineapple cubes
maraschino cherries

If the ham or gammon has been hung for a long time and is very dry and salty, soak it for 24 hours at least, changing the water every 6–8 hours. For most hams, about 12 hours' soaking or less is enough.

To calculate the cooking time, drain the ham, then weigh it and measure its thickness. The cooking time will be divided between boiling and roasting, so calculate the time for both methods. The ham should be boiled for 20 minutes per 450 g/1 lb of meat. For the subsequent roasting, allow 30 minutes per 450 g/1 lb of meat, plus 30 minutes over, for any joint more than 10 cm/4 in thick.

Clean and trim off any 'rusty' parts. Put the ham into a boiling pot big enough to hold it, but keep the knuckle end out of the water so you can use it to handle the joint. Add enough cold water to cover the joint, and cover the pan with a cloth to prevent undue evaporation. Heat to simmering point and simmer gently for the required time.

Pre-heat the oven to 200°C/400°F/gas 6.

Lift out the ham and remove the rind. Lay out three thicknesses of aluminium foil, and place the ham in the centre. Fold the foil over to enclose the ham completely. Put the ham in a baking tin and bake for 15 minutes. Reduce the heat to 150°C/300°F/gas 2 for the rest of the calculated cooking time.

When cooked, remove from the oven and carefully take off the covering. Raise the oven heat to 220°C/425°F/gas 7. Score the fat in a pattern of squares, then brush it all over with the apricot jam. Arrange pineapple cubes and maraschino cherries at regular intervals on the ham. Brush over with a little more jam. Cook, uncovered, in the hot oven for 5–8 minutes until the glaze is set. Serve hot or cold.

STANDARD CHRISTMAS PUDDING

100 g/4 oz plain flour
25 g/1 oz self-raising flour
pinch of salt
100 g/4 oz day-old white breadcrumbs
1 cooking apple, chopped
100 g/4 oz mixed dried fruit
100 g/4 oz soft dark brown sugar
200 g/7 oz shredded suet
150 g/5 oz cut mixed peel
grated rind and juice of 1 lemon
2 eggs
about 125 ml/4½ fl oz milk
1 × 5 ml spoon/1 tsp almond essence
1 × 5 ml spoon/1 tsp gravy browning
fat for greasing

Grease two 600 ml/1 pt basins or one 1 litre/1¾ pt basin. Sift together the flours and salt into a bowl. Add the breadcrumbs, apple, dried fruit, sugar, suet, peel, lemon rind and juice.

Beat together the eggs, milk and almond essence and stir into the dry ingredients, adding more milk if needed to give a soft dropping consistency. Add the gravy browning to darken the mixture, and mix thoroughly.

Fill the mixture into the basin or basins. Cover with greased paper and a scalded and floured cloth (for boiling) or with greased paper or foil (for steaming), and boil or half-steam for 5 hours (see p. 32). Cover with clean greaseproof paper and a clean, dry cloth, and store in a cool place.

To reheat, boil or half-steam for 1½–2 hours.

MAKES 2 6-PORTION OR 1 12-PORTION PUDDING

To cover a pudding

Pack the basin with the mixture leaving at least 2.5 cm/1 in headspace to allow for the pudding to rise.

Cover with greased paper or foil, greased side down, to prevent any steam getting in. Either twist the edge under the rim of the basin or tie tightly with string.

To steam a pudding

Put the pudding in the perforated top part and keep the water at a gentle, rolling boil.

If you do not have a steamer, stand the pudding basin on an inverted old saucer or plate in a saucepan, with water coming halfway up the sides of the basin. Cover the pan with a tight-fitting lid and simmer gently. This method is known as 'half-steaming'.

With either method, always add more boiling water when the level has reduced by a third.

To turn out the pudding

Once cooked, allow the pudding to stand for a few minutes. Remove the cloth and paper or foil, and run a knife round the sides of the bowl to loosen the pudding. Place the warmed, upturned serving dish over the bowl, and turn them over together. If the pudding does not come free, give the dish and bowl a sharp sideways shake.

BRANDY BUTTER

200 g/7 oz icing sugar, sifted
100 g/4 oz unsalted butter, softened
1–2 × 15 ml spoons/1–2 tbsp brandy

Cream the butter, and gradually beat in the sugar until the mixture is pale and light. Add the brandy to taste a few drops at a time, beating well. Take care that the mixture does not separate.

Chill before using.

MAKES 325 G/11 OZ.

CREAM CUSTARD SAUCE

4 eggs
100 g/4 oz caster sugar
250 ml/8 fl oz milk
grated rind of 2 oranges
250 ml/8 fl oz single cream

Beat together the eggs, sugar and milk. Add the orange rind and cream.

Pour the mixture into a double boiler or a bowl placed over a pan of simmering water. Cook, stirring constantly, until the sauce thickens. It must not boil, or the sauce will curdle.

Serve hot or cold.

MAKES ABOUT 500 ML/18 FL OZ

CHRISTMAS CAKE

CHRISTMAS CAKE

fat for greasing the tin
200 g/7 oz plain flour
large pinch of salt
1 × 5 ml spoon/1 tsp ground cinnamon
½ × 5 ml spoon/½ tsp grated nutmeg
½ × 5 ml spoon/½ tsp ground ginger
100 g/4 oz glacé cherries, quartered
100 g/4 oz mixed peel
200 g/7 oz sultanas
200 g/7 oz currants
200 g/7 oz raisins
50 g/2 oz blanched almonds, chopped
50 g/2 oz ground almonds
200 g/7 oz butter
200 g/7 oz soft brown sugar
5 eggs, beaten
2–4 × 15 ml spoons/2–4 tbsp brandy or sherry

Grease and line a 20 cm/8 in cake tin with double greaseproof paper, and place a double strip of brown paper or newspaper round the outside of the tin. Pre-heat the oven to 170°C/325°F/gas 3.

Sift the flour, salt and spices together into a bowl. Transfer one third of this flour mixture to another bowl and mix with the fruit, nuts and ground almonds.

Cream the butter and sugar together until light and fluffy. Gradually beat the eggs into the creamed mixture, beating thoroughly after each addition. If the mixture curdles, mix in a little of the flour mixture. Fold in the remaining flour, salt and spices, and then the cherries and mixed peel, dried fruit and almonds. Then add the brandy or sherry and mix well.

Transfer the mixture to the prepared tin. Make the top as smooth and flat as possible, and then make a slight hollow in the centre.

Bake for 45 minutes, then reduce the heat to 150°C/300°F/gas 2 and bake for a further hour. Reduce the heat again, to 140°C/275°F/gas 1, for a further 45 minutes to 1 hour. The cake is cooked when it is firm to the touch and is beginning to come away from the sides of the tin. A skewer stuck into the centre of the cake should come out clean.

Leave the cake to cool in the tin. Then turn it out and carefully peel away all the greaseproof paper. When it is completely cold, wrap in a double layer of clean greaseproof paper and then in aluminium foil.

HANDLING THE CAKE

Once the cake is covered in almond paste or icing it becomes difficult to pick up and move. Take a strip of kitchen foil or greaseproof paper, roughly double the diameter of the cake in width and about three times the diameter of the cake in length. Fold the strip in half lengthways, and in half lengthways again to make a strip that is strong enough to bear the weight of the cake. Before beginning to cover the cake, place it on the strip of paper/foil so that you can hold the ends of the strip and use it to lift the cake. Leave it under the cake all the time so that it is in position whenever you need to lift the cake. When the cake is finally iced and decorated and in position on a cake-board or plate, gently pull the paper/foil away from under it. This is also a useful device for getting a cake into and out of a tight-fitting tin.

TO COVER THE CAKE WITH ALMOND PASTE

Any fruit cake that is going to be iced needs a layer of almond paste to act as a barrier between the two, to prevent crumbs being picked up when the icing is spread over the cake, and to prevent the cake discolouring the icing – both of which can make the finished cake look dirty and unattractive. It also gives a flat, smooth surface for icing, making it easier to get a good finish. If your family does not like almond paste, roll it out thinly.

The cake should be brushed with a thin coat of apricot glaze first, as this will hold the almond paste to the cake when the cake is cut.

Apricot glaze
  250 g/9 oz apricot jam
  3 × 15 ml spoons/3 tbsp water

Heat the jam and water gently in a saucepan until smooth.

Sieve the mixture and return to a clean saucepan. Bring slowly to the boil and heat gently until thick.

Almond paste
  300 g/11 oz ground almonds
  300–450 g/11 oz–1 lb icing sugar
  2 egg yolks or 2 egg whites or 1 egg

Work all the ingredients together to make a pliable paste. Handle it as little as possible, because the warmth of the hands draws out the oil from the ground almonds.

Makes enough for the top and sides of a 20 cm/8 in cake.

Quantities of almond paste

Keeping the same proportions, you will need the following quantities of the ingredients for different sizes of cake.

TO COVER THE TOP ONLY:
☆ 18 cm/7¼ in cake = 100 g/4 oz ground almonds etc
☆ 20–23 cm/8–9¼ in cake = 150 g/5 oz ground almonds, etc
☆ 25 cm/10 in cake = 200 g/7 oz ground almonds, etc

TO COVER THE TOP AND SIDES:
☆ 18 cm/7¼ in cake = 200 g/7 oz ground almonds, etc
☆ 20–23 cm/8–9¼ in cake = 300 g/11 oz ground almonds, etc
☆ 25 cm/10 in cake = 400 g/14 oz ground almonds, etc

Ready-made almond paste

If you are using ready-made almond paste, look for a type that feels soft in the packet and knead it well before use. You will need 680 g/1½ lb to cover the top and sides of a 20 cm/8 in cake.

To cover the cake

First level the top of the cake by cutting a thin strip of paste and positioning it around the edge of the cake. Press flat.

TO COVER THE TOP ONLY OF A ROUND OR SQUARE CAKE:
Dust the work surface with icing sugar. Roll out the almond paste to a square or round of the preferred thickness, allowing an extra 5 mm/¼ in all round. Take the cake and place it upside down in the centre of the paste. Hold the cake in place with one hand, and press the paste against the edge of the cake, working to get a good sharp edge. Turn the cake the right way up. If the top is not flat, roll lightly until it is, then turn the cake

upside down again and press excess paste against the sides. Turn the right way up again. If the sides are lumpy and uneven, roll a milk bottle or jamjar around the side of the cake.

Leave for a minimum of three days, and preferably a week, to harden before icing.

TO COVER THE TOP AND SIDES OF A ROUND CAKE:
Roll out the paste to the preferred thickness, and about 3–4 cm/1⅛ in–1¾ in larger than the top of the cake. If the cake is very deep, make the circles a little bigger. Turn the cake upside down and position it in the centre of the paste. Press and mould the paste into the sides of the cake, making sure to create a sharp, neat edge around the top of the cake. Roll a milk bottle round the sides to smooth the paste against the cake.

TO COVER THE TOP AND SIDES OF A SQUARE CAKE:
Cover the sides first. Divide the paste in half. Take one half and divide into four pieces. Roll out each to fit the sides of the cake. Turn the cake on to one side and press each side in turn on to a strip of paste. Trim away any excess paste to create neat edges.

To cover the top, follow the instructions for covering the top only.

TO ICE THE CAKE

First decide on the style of decoration: rough, which is quick and simple; or smooth, which is time-consuming and requires a little experience of cake decorating.

Royal icing

2 egg whites
450 kg/1 lb icing sugar
1 × 5 ml spoon/1 tsp lemon juice

Put the egg whites and lemon juice into a bowl and, using a wooden spoon, beat just enough to liquefy the whites slightly.

Add half the icing sugar a little at a time, and beat for 10 minutes. Add the rest of the icing sugar gradually and beat for another 10 minutes, until the icing is white and forms peaks when the spoon is drawn up from the mixture.

This quantity will be enough to cover the top and sides of a 20 cm/8 in cake: use half this quantity for the top only. For a 25 cm/10 in cake, double the quantities given above so as to cover the top and sides.

ROUGH FINISH:
The simplest form of decoration is a snow-scene effect. You can achieve this by spreading the icing over the cake with a knife (a palette knife if you have one), and pulling it into rough peaks once you have covered the cake. Cake decorations such as fir trees, igloos and robins can be positioned in the icing at this stage, and the cake can be sprinkled with sifted icing sugar to look like snow. (If the icing sticks to your knife too much, dip the knife into hot water.)

A more elaborate scene can be created by using almond paste under the icing to build up constructions such as hills or toboggan runs, and you can add figures tobogganing, skiing or having a snowball fight. The appropriate figures can be bought, or they can be moulded out of ready-made fondant icing and left to harden.

SMOOTH FINISH:
Those who feel more ambitious, or who can afford to spend more time on decorating the cake, can cover the cake with two smooth layers of icing and decorate it with piping, or with coloured, cut-out shapes made from

almond paste or fondant icing, or with a combination of the two.

First coat: Place the cake on an icing turntable or an upturned plate. Put almost half the icing in the centre of the cake and smooth it out to the sides with a knife that has been dipped in hot water. Spread the rest of the icing round the sides of the cake. Aim for a smooth surface to the icing, and a clean, sharp corner all around the top of the cake, but do not overwork the icing. Leave for a minimum of 24 hours (the cake can be left up to a week before the second coat).

Second coat: The second coat should be thinner than the first so that it will almost pour on to the cake. Additional egg white in the icing will make it extra-smooth. Draw the edge of a palette knife across the top of the cake to get an absolutely smooth flat finish. Then hold the palette knife against the side of the cake, and either revolve the cake (if on an icing turntable) or hold the knife vertically and run it round the sides to get them as smooth and even as possible. Decorations can then be piped on to the cake, or it can be decorated with coloured marzipan shapes.

PIPING:

Plan your pattern carefully first, drawing it out on a piece of paper the same size as the top of the cake. You can prick out the pattern in the icing if you do not feel confident of doing it freehand. Useful templates can be bought in shops that sell cooking equipment.

Instead of a complicated piped pattern, you could write a Christmas message in different-coloured icing across the top of the cake.

MARZIPAN SHAPES:

Knead the marzipan and then colour it by taking up a little edible food colouring on a cocktail stick and adding it to the marzipan. Add a little colouring at a time as it is quite strong, and keep adding more until you get the depth of colour you want. Knead the marzipan again until the colouring is evenly distributed, and then roll it out thinly. Cut out the shapes with a sharp knife or special cutters – holly leaves, bows, bells, etc. Use a little icing to fix them in position on top of the cake.

You will need a proper cakeboard on which to stand the cake, unless you have an extra-large plate, as the cake will probably be too big for a dinner plate. Transfer the cake onto the cakeboard.

Finishing off

If you have iced only the top you will need a cake frill to cover the sides. Or you could cover them with chopped nuts – coat the sides of the cake with apricot glaze (see p. 35), scoop up the chopped nuts on a palette knife and press them against the sides of the cake.

If the whole cake is covered in smooth icing, you could just tie a length of ribbon around the cake. Or use two pieces of ribbon, in different colours and widths, the narrower one placed on top of the wider one.

If the whole cake has been covered with rough icing, the sides can be left plain.

CHRISTMAS BAKING

MINCE PIES

shortcrust pastry using 275 g/10 oz flour; other pastries such as flaky or filo pastry are also good
flour for rolling out
250 g/9 oz mincemeat (see opposite)
25 g/1 oz caster sugar or icing sugar for dredging

Pre-heat the oven to 230°C/450°F/gas 8.

Roll out the pastry to 3 mm/⅛ in thick on a lightly floured surface, and use just over half to line twelve 7 cm/2¾ in patty tins. Cut out twelve lids from the rest of the pastry.

Place a spoonful of mincemeat in each pastry case. Moisten the edges of the pastry lids. Seal the edges well, brush the tops with water and dredge with sugar. Make two small cuts in the top of each pie.

Reduce the oven temperature to 200°C/400°F/gas 6 and bake the mince pies for 15–20 minutes.

MAKES 12

MINCEMEAT

200 g/7 oz cut mixed peel, chopped
200 g/7 oz raisins
200 g/7 oz preserved ginger, chopped
200 g/7 oz cooking apples, grated
200 g/7 oz shredded suet (beef or vegetable)
200 g/7 oz sultanas
200 g/7 oz currants
200 g/7 oz soft light brown sugar
50 g/2 oz blanched almonds, chopped
large pinch of mixed spice
large pinch of ground ginger
large pinch of ground cinnamon
grated rind and juice of 2 lemons
grated rind and juice of 1 orange
150 ml/¼ pt cherry or brandy or rum

Combine all the ingredients in a large bowl. Cover and leave for two days, stirring occasionally. (This prevents fermentation later.) Pot in sterilized jars, cover with waxed discs and screw-on lids, and label. Store in a cool, dry place.

MAKES ABOUT 1.8 KG/3½ LB

BÛCHE DE NOËL (CHESTNUT CHRISTMAS LOG)

SPONGE:
butter for greasing
100 g/4 oz icing sugar
3 eggs
4 × 5 ml spoons/4 tsp rum
65 g/2½ oz self-raising flour
icing sugar for dusting

FILLING:
2 × 440 g/15 oz cans unsweetened chestnut puree
275 g/10 oz butter, softened
125 g/4½ oz caster sugar
2 × 15 ml spoons/2 tbsp rum

DECORATION:
marrons glâcés or glacé cherries and angelica

Grease a 35 × 25 cm/14 × 10 in Swiss roll tin and line it with greased paper. Pre-heat the oven at 220°C/425°F/gas 7.

Warm a mixing bowl with hot water, then dry it. Sift the icing sugar into the bowl, and break in the eggs. Beat or whisk vigorously for 5–10 minutes until the mixture is very light and fluffy, adding the rum while beating. When the mixture is like meringue, fold in the flour gently. Turn the mixture into the prepared tin, and bake for 7 minutes. Meanwhile, prepare a 40 × 30 cm/16 × 10 in sheet of greaseproof paper and dust it with icing sugar. Remove the sponge from the oven, loosen the sides from the tin if necessary, and turn it on to the greaseproof paper. Peel off the lining paper. Trim the edges of the sponge if they are crisp. Roll it up tightly with the greaseproof paper, beginning at one long side to make a long thin roll, or at one short end for a shorter roll. Cool.

Meanwhile, prepare the chestnut butter cream for the filling. Turn the puree into a bowl and beat in the butter, then add the sugar and rum.

When the sponge is cold, unroll it carefully. Cover the underside of the sponge with just over half the butter cream, laying it on thickly at the further edge. Then reroll the sponge and place it on a sheet of greaseproof paper, with the cut edge underneath. Cover the sponge log with the remaining butter cream, either spreading with a knife or using a piping bag with a ribbon nozzle, and imitating the knots and grain of wood. Chill, and serve decorated with glacé fruits.

SERVES 6–8

PÂTÉS AND TERRINES

PÂTÉ MAISON

3 bay leaves
8–10 back bacon rashers, rinds removed
100 g/4 oz pig's liver, trimmed
100 g/4 oz fresh belly of pork, skinned and trimmed
200 g/7 oz cold, cooked rabbit pieces
200 g/7 oz pork sausagemeat
1 onion, chopped
25 g/1 oz fresh white breadcrumbs
1 egg
1 × 15 ml spoon/1 tbsp milk
5 × 15 ml/5 tbsp brandy
salt and pepper

Pre-heat the oven to 180°C/350°F/gas 4.

Put the bay leaves in the base of a 1.25 litre/2 pt oblong ovenproof dish. Line the dish with the bacon rashers, reserving two or three to cover the top.

Chop the liver, pork and rabbit coarsely and mix with the sausagemeat. Add the onion and breadcrumbs to the mixture. If you have a blender you can process these ingredients to a coarse paste.

Beat together the egg, milk and brandy. Work into the dry ingredients and season to taste.

Turn the mixture into the lined dish, cover with the reserved bacon rashers and then with a lid or foil. Stand the dish in a pan with hot water to come halfway up its sides. Cook the pâté in the oven for 1 hour.

When cooked, put a heavy weight on the pâté and leave to cool. To serve, remove the bacon rashers from the top and turn out of the dish.

MAKES ABOUT 1 KG/2¼ LB

CHICKEN LIVER PÂTÉ

100 g/4 oz slightly salted butter
1 small onion, chopped
1 garlic clove, crushed
450 g/1 lb chicken livers, trimmed
3 × 15 ml spoons/3 tbsp brandy
1 × 15 ml spoon/1 tbsp port or Madeira
2 × 5 ml spoons/2 tsp French mustard
pinch of ground mace
pinch of ground cloves
salt and pepper
3 × 15 ml spoons/3 tbsp aspic jelly or jellied canned consommé

Melt 50 g/2 oz of the butter in a large frying pan. Add the onion and garlic and fry gently until softened but not coloured. Add the chicken livers to the pan and fry, turning them frequently, for about 6 minutes until browned but not crisp.

Scrape the contents of the pan into a bowl. Pour the brandy and port or Madeira into the frying pan, stir well and then add to the chicken liver mixture. Add the remaining butter, the mustard and spices and season well. Mash or pound and then sieve the mixture, or puree in a blender or processor to a smooth paste.

Turn the pâté into an earthenware dish or pot, leaving 1 cm/½ in headroom. Cover loosely with greaseproof paper and leave in the refrigerator or a cool place until firm.

Meanwhile, melt the aspic jelly or consommé and let it cool until almost setting. Spoon it over the pâté and leave in the refrigerator or a cool place to set for at least 24 hours.

Serve the pâté the same day, or store it in the freezer.

MAKES ABOUT 1.5 KG/3 LB

TERRINE OF DUCK

450 g/1 lb raw boneless duck meat
100 ml/4 fl oz brandy
2 shallots
200 g/7 oz belly of pork, skinned and trimmed
275 g/10 oz raw chicken meat, skinned
shredded rind of 1 orange
pinch of dried thyme
pinch of dried savory
salt and pepper
3 eggs, beaten
450 g/1 lb streaky bacon rashers, rinds removed
3 bay leaves

Pre-heat the oven to 180°C/350°F/gas 4.

Mince or grind the duck meat and put it in a bowl with the brandy. Stir well, cover and leave for 4–5 hours.

Chop the shallots and mince the pork and chicken, or process in a blender. Stir in the orange rind, herbs and seasonings, and finally the eggs. Mix thoroughly.

Line a 1.5 litre/3 pt ovenproof dish with the bacon rashers, reserving enough to cover the top. Press in the meat mixture, level the top and arrange the bay leaves in the centre. Cover with the reserved bacon, then with foil. Stand the dish in a pan of hot water to come halfway up its sides.

Cook the terrine for 1 hour, or until it has begun to shrink slightly from the sides of the dish. Remove the foil and the bacon and return the terrine to the oven for 15 minutes to brown it slightly.

Put a weight on the cooked terrine and, when it is cool, store in the refrigerator for at least 12 hours. Serve it, cut in slices, from the dish.

MAKES ABOUT 1.5 KG/3 LB

EDIBLE PRESENTS

FLORENTINES

fat for greasing
25 g/1 oz glacé cherries, chopped
100 g/4 oz cut mixed peel, finely chopped
50 g/2 oz flaked almonds
100 g/4 oz chopped almonds
25 g/1 oz sultanas
100 g/4 oz butter or margarine
100 g/4 oz caster sugar
30 ml/2 tbsp double cream
100 g/4 oz plain or couverture chocolate

Line three or four baking sheets with oiled greaseproof paper. Pre-heat the oven to 180°C/350°F/gas 4.

In a bowl, mix the cherries and mixed peel with the flaked and chopped almonds and the sultanas. Melt the butter or margarine in a small saucepan, add the sugar and boil for 1 minute. Remove from the heat and stir in the fruit and nut mixture. Whip the cream in a separate bowl, then fold it in.

Place small spoonfuls of the mixture on to the

prepared baking sheets, leaving room for spreading. Bake for 8–10 minutes. After the biscuits have been cooking for about 5 minutes, neaten the edges by drawing them together with a plain biscuit cutter. Leave the cooked biscuits on the baking sheets to firm up slightly before transferring to a wire rack to cool completely.

To finish, melt the chocolate in a bowl over hot water and use to coat the flat underside of each biscuit. Mark into wavy lines with a fork as the chocolate cools.

MAKES 20–24

GINGERBREAD SHAPES

225 g/8 oz self-raising flour
1 × 2.5 ml spoon/½ tsp salt
1 × 5 ml spoon/1 tsp mixed spice
2 × 5 ml spoons/2 tsp ground ginger
100 g/4 oz margarine
75 g/3 oz soft light brown sugar
3 × 15 ml spoons/3 tbsp milk, plus extra for brushing

Pre-heat the oven to 200°C/400°F/gas 6.

Sift the flour, salt and spices into a mixing bowl. Rub in the margarine until it is evenly mixed. Stir in the sugar and milk and mix to a fairly stiff dough.

Roll out the dough on a lightly floured board. Cut into decorative shapes – men, stars, Christmas trees – with cutters or by hand. Gather up the trimmings, shape them into a ball, roll out the dough and cut out more biscuits. Place the biscuit shapes on a greased baking sheet and brush them lightly with milk.

Bake for 15 minutes, or until the biscuits are golden brown. Transfer them to a wire rack and leave them to cool.

CLEMENTINES IN VODKA

1 kg/2¼ lb clementines
100 g/4 oz caster sugar
600 ml/1 pt water
½ vanilla pod
2 × 15 ml spoons/2 tbsp orange flower water
300 ml/½ pt vodka

Remove the leaves, stalks and flower ends from the clementines. Prick them all over with a darning needle – this helps the syrup to penetrate the skins.

Put the sugar, water and vanilla pod in a saucepan over a low heat, and stir occasionally. When the sugar has dissolved, add the clementines, increase the heat, bring to the boil and simmer, uncovered, for about 25 minutes, until the fruit is tender. Remove the vanilla pod.

Drain the fruit, reserving the syrup. Pack the fruit into two warm sterilized jars. Divide the vodka between them, then fill up the jars with the syrup. Seal the jars and up-end them gently to blend the liquids.

FILLS 2 × 700 G/2 LB JARS

CHOCOLATE FUDGE

oil for greasing
400 g/14 oz granulated sugar
50 g/2 oz golden syrup
50 g/2 oz butter
25 g/1 oz cocoa powder
75 ml/3 fl oz milk
50 ml/2 fl oz single cream

Grease a 15 cm/6 in square tin.

Put all the ingredients into a heavy saucepan and

dissolve the sugar gently. Bring to the boil and boil to the soft ball stage (the mixture will roll into a soft ball that can be squeezed between the fingers), stirring all the time. Cool for 5 minutes, then beat until creamy and matt in appearance. Pour the mixture into the prepared tin. Leave until cold before cutting into squares. Pack and store in an airtight tin lined with waxed paper.

MAKES APPROX. 500 G/18 OZ

CHOCOLATE TRUFFLES

50 g/2 oz almonds, chopped
100 g/4 oz plain chocolate
100 g/4 oz ground almonds
2 × 15 ml spoons/2 tbsp double cream
75 g/3 oz caster sugar
few drops of vanilla essence
grated chocolate or chocolate vermicelli for coating

Brown the chopped almonds lightly under the grill. Break the chocolate into small pieces and melt it in a bowl over a pan of hot water. Remove the bowl from the pan. Add all the other ingredients except the coating chocolate and mix to a stiff paste. Roll into small balls, and toss at once in grated chocolate or chocolate vermicelli.

Put the truffles into paper sweet cases to serve.

MAKES ABOUT 24

PEPPERMINT CREAMS

400 g/14 oz icing sugar
2 egg whites
2 × 5 ml spoons/2 tsp peppermint essence
icing sugar for dusting

Sift the icing sugar into a bowl, and work in the egg whites and peppermint essence. Mix well to a moderately firm paste. Knead thoroughly and roll out, on a board dusted with a little icing sugar, to about 6 mm/¼ in thick. Cut into small rounds or fancy shapes and put on greaseproof paper.

Leave to dry for 12 hours, turning each sweet once. Pack in an airtight container lined with waxed paper.

The sweets may be dipped, or half-dipped, in melted couverture chocolate.

MAKES ABOUT 48

Chapter 4

CHRISTMAS DRINKS

As with the food, you should plan your Christmas drinks requirements in advance – for before and after meals, for wines to go with the meals, and of course for any entertaining that you are planning to do.

You can buy the Christmas drinks in advance of the pre-Christmas rush if you have somewhere cool and out of the way to store them, such as the corner of the garage or a cellar. If you do not have anywhere to store a quantity of drink, you can put in an order at the local off-licence about a month ahead and pick it all up just before Christmas. This way you know you will get what you want. It is also possible to order wine by the case (often with a discount) at some supermarkets.

If you are giving a party and will need to hire glasses it is well worth buying the drinks at an off-licence, because in this case many off-licences will not charge for the hire of glasses, only for breakages.

CHOOSING WINE TO ACCOMPANY FOOD

When selecting wine to go with a meal, as good a rule as any is to choose one that you know you like. However, a useful rough guideline to follow is to match the dryness/sweetness and strength of flavour of the wine to that of the food it is to be served with. For example, a strongly flavoured meat dish, or game, should be matched with a full-flavoured red, whereas the subtle flavour of poultry is better accompanied by a lighter red or a robust white. Fish, which is usually delicate in flavour, is best accompanied by white or rosé. With sweet food dry wines can taste very bitter, and light dry wines become flavourless. Rich, sweet desserts are best matched by a sweet, fruity white, whereas light desserts are best with a sweet, light wine.

If you are not sure what to get, don't be afraid to ask for advice. In off-licences, staff will always help – often all you need to do is tell them what you are serving and they will suggest a suitable wine to accompany it. Off-licences and supermarkets often also provide good written descriptions of individual wines on the shelves.

WINES FOR CHRISTMAS DINNER

Before the meal:	Serve a light aperitif to whet the appetite – dry sherry, or, if you are feeling extravagant, chilled champagne or sparkling wine.
First course, cold and fish dishes:	Dry or medium white or rosé (Muscadet, Pouilly Fumé, Chablis, Vouvray, Rosé d'Anjou).*
Smoked salmon, consommé:	Chilled dry sherry, chilled white port.
Turkey:	Red – a good-quality claret, fruity Rioja, or a Côtes du Rhone or medium Italian such as Bardolino. White – white Burgundy, or a dry, fruity Loire or German wine.
Goose:	A full-bodied red, such as a Burgundy or Barolo.

Pudding:	A dessert wine (Sauternes, a German Auslese or Spätlese, Monbazillac from the Bergerac region of France, or Muscat de Beaumes de Venise).*
Cheese etc:	Port.

* A separate wine for the first course, and a dessert wine, are optional. You might prefer to offer a choice of a white and a red throughout the meal instead.

HOW MUCH PER PERSON?

It is usual to allow three glasses of wine per person; i.e. one white with the first course, and two red or another white with the main course. If you are serving a dessert wine, allow one glass per person. A standard bottle of wine gives six to eight glasses.

For a meal that is likely to last a long time, it is a good idea to have one or two extra bottles in reserve.

WHAT TEMPERATURE?

Wines taste much better if they are served at the correct temperature.

☆ *Dry white, sparkling*: chilled – 10–12°C/50–54°F.
☆ *Rosé, dessert wines*: lightly chilled – 14°C/57°F.
☆ *Light reds* (e.g. Beaujolais): cool room temperature – 15–16°C/59–61°F.
☆ *Fine clarets, full-bodied reds* (e.g. Burgundies, and Italian, Spanish and Californian red wines): average room temperature – 16–20°C/61–68°F.

PORT

Traditionally served with cheese, port can continue to be drunk with the nuts and sweetmeats at the end of the meal. It ranges from dry to sweet, and vintage port is invariably very expensive. 'Late bottled' port is better, and only slightly more expensive, than standard port.

Port is passed clockwise round the table, and everyone pours their own. Etiquette requires that the bottle/decanter is not put down on the table until it has completed the round.

DECANTING

Fine red wines and vintage port need to be decanted in order to separate the wine from the sediment that will have collected at the bottom of the bottle. The process of decanting also allows the wine to 'breathe', thus bringing out its full flavour.

As you pour the wine or port from the bottle into a decanter or wine jug hold it against the light so that you can see when you have reached the sediment. If the wine has a very heavy sediment, it can be strained through a piece of clean, fine muslin.

CHRISTMAS DRINKS CHECKLIST

- champagne
- sparkling wine
- red table wine
- white table wine
- sweet dessert wine
- sherry
- port
- liqueurs
- ice – consider buying packs of ice in order to make sure that you don't run out over the holiday
- hire of glasses
- brandy
- spirits
- beer/lager
- cider
- low-alcohol wine
- low-alcohol beer
- mixers

RECIPES FOR SOME FAVOURITE CHRISTMAS DRINKS

PUNCHES

MULLED WINE

500 ml/18 fl oz water
6 cloves
½ cinnamon stick, lightly crushed
pinch of grated nutmeg
thinly pared rind of ½ lemon
1 bottle (70–75 cl/1¼ pt) claret
granulated sugar

Put the water into an enamel or stainless steel saucepan and heat gently. Stir in the spices and lemon rind. Heat to boiling point and simmer for 10 minutes. Strain the liquid into a bowl and add the wine. Sweeten to taste with sugar.

Return the liquid to the pan and heat without boiling. Serve immediately.

FILLS 10 WINEGLASSES

WHISKY PUNCH

thinly pared rind and juice of 3 lemons
1 litre/1¾ pt boiling water
1 bottle (75 cl/1¼ pt) whisky
200 g/7 oz lump sugar

Strain the lemon juice and put it into a bowl with the lemon rind. Pour the boiling water over it, then add the whisky and stir in the sugar. When the sugar is dissolved, strain the liquid and serve at once.

FILLS 15 WINEGLASSES

HOT RUM TODDY

2 × 5 ml spoons/2 tsp Demerara sugar or to taste
juice of 1 lemon
50 ml/2 fl oz rum
2 lemon slices
boiling water

Mix the sugar with the lemon juice and rum. Put 1 lemon slice into each of 2 heated mugs, and pour half the rum mixture into each mug. Add boiling water to give the desired strength of toddy. Taste, and add extra sugar if needed. Serve at once, as hot as possible.

FILLS 2 MUGS

NON-ALCOHOLIC FRUIT PUNCH

1 litre/1¾ pt red grape juice
thinly pared rind and juice of 3 oranges
6 cloves
4 cm/1½ in piece cinnamon stick, lightly crushed
granulated sugar
2 eating apples, thinly sliced

Put the grape juice, orange rind and juice and spices into an enamel or stainless steel saucepan and heat to boiling point. Simmer over a low heat for 10 minutes. Add the sugar and stir occasionally until it has dissolved. Strain the liquid and discard the orange rind and spices.

Add the apple slices, and serve immediately.

FILLS 10 WINEGLASSES

COCKTAILS

BLOODY MARY

ice cubes
1 part vodka
2 parts tomato juice
a few drops Worcestershire sauce
a few drops fresh lemon juice
salt and pepper

Put the ice cubes in a medium-sized glass. Stir or shake all the ingredients together, and pour over the ice.

BUCKS FIZZ

juice of 1 orange
chilled dry champagne

Strain the orange juice and chill it. Pour into a champage glass and top up with the champagne. Do not add ice.

CHAMPAGNE COCKTAIL

1 lump of sugar
a few drops of Angostura bitters
1 × 5 ml/1 tsp spoon brandy
chilled champagne
1 slice orange

Put a lump of sugar in a champagne glass and soak it in the Angostura bitters. Add the brandy and top up with chilled champagne. Place the orange slice on top.

Chapter 5

ENTERTAINING

The thought of trying to give a party on top of providing Christmas for the family may make you feel exhausted before you start. But entertaining and seeing friends are important aspects of Christmas for most people, and by applying the same kind of planning as you do for Christmas itself, it should be possible. As with the general preparations, it really is worth planning well ahead. That will enable you to integrate shopping, cooking and other preparations with those for the rest of Christmas.

WHAT TYPE OF PARTY?

Decide as early as possible what type of party you are going to give – drinks, buffet, or a lunch or dinner party. If you have small children or teenagers, do you want to give one for them? Consider the number of guests you can happily cope with. How much space have you got? Will you have enough glasses, cutlery, serving dishes, etc., for the number you want to invite? Do you have the facilities to prepare and serve food for a large number?

When deciding on the date, consider whether the Christmas holiday itself is best, or whether slightly before or after Christmas would be better. Do you want it to tie in with when you will have guests staying? Are there any other factors that you should take into account?

DRINKS PARTIES

DRINKS

It is quite usual to offer a limited selection of drinks, or even just a choice of red and white wine, in order to simplify the serving. However, if you wish to offer a range of drinks, you can choose from the following:

☆ *gin* – with tonic water, bitter lemon, lime juice, dry vermouth, plus ice and a slice of lemon
☆ *rum*, white or dark – with lime juice, orange juice, lemonade or cola
☆ *vermouth*, sweet or dry – with tonic water, orange juice or lemonade, plus a slice of lemon or orange
☆ *vodka* – with tonic, lime juice or orange juice, plus ice
☆ *whisky* – with water, soda water or ginger ale, plus ice
☆ *white wine* – with soda water, chilled.

Or you could offer mulled wine, a wine punch or one or more cocktails (see pp. 55–7). In either of these cases, it is a good idea to offer sherry as an alternative for those who do not want something too strong or unusual.
Remember to have plenty of soft drinks for drivers and other non-drinkers.
See p. 54 for a full checklist.

A *guide to quantities*

	Glasses per standard bottle
Spirits	24
Allow 8–10 small bottles of mixers to each bottle of spirits	
Sherry	16

Table wine	6–8
Tomato juice (600 ml/1 pt carton)	4–6
Fruit juice (600 ml/1 pt carton)	4
Fruit cordial (allowing 4 litres/7 pt water to each bottle)	20–25
Fruit squash (allowing 2.5 litres/4 pt water to each bottle)	14–18

Allow about three to four glasses for those who are not driving. Drivers may have one or two alcoholic drinks and then move on to soft drinks, or they may avoid alcohol altogether. You could consider mixing a fruit punch for those who have to drive, rather than just serving plain fruit juice.

FOOD

In planning the food, try to have a mix of light and more solid eats. Avoid things that take lots of last-minute preparation and decorating. Trays of canapés or little biscuits spread with delicious toppings and delicate decorations look marvellous, but take hours to prepare.

Items such as vol-au-vent cases, sausage rolls and cocktail sausages can be bought frozen well in advance and cooked straight from the freezer. Or you can make your own pastry. Little choux pastry balls can be made in advance and frozen. Defrost on the day, and fill with a cream cheese or fish filling.

ABOUT ONE MONTH AHEAD

☆ Send out invitations
☆ Order drinks, and arrange hire of glasses if needed.

LAST-MINUTE PREPARATIONS

☆ Make space in the fridge or freezer for cooling drinks

☆ Buy extra ice
☆ Collect drinks and glasses
☆ Clear room
☆ Put out drinks
☆ Put out food
☆ Put out glasses – allow time for washing them if they are hired
☆ Distribute several ashtrays around the room.

BUFFET PARTIES

FOOD

Keep the food easy to prepare, and easy to finish off and serve. Plan dishes that can be cooked or part-cooked in advance and frozen, such as pâtés, stews and casseroles. Or you could plan a theme menu, such as Indian. A cold buffet may appear to be easier to produce than a hot meal, but a range of different salads, involving lots of chopping and arranging, takes deceptively long to prepare and has to be done almost at the last minute.

If you are cooking for a large number, check that you have enough dishes in which to serve the meal.

DRINKS

Wine and/or beer and soft drinks are the easiest to serve to a large number of people. See p. 54 for a full checklist and see above for a guide to quantities.

ABOUT ONE MONTH AHEAD

☆ Send out invitations
☆ Order drinks, and arrange hire of glasses if needed.

LAST-MINUTE PREPARATIONS

☆ Make space in the fridge or freezer for cooling drinks
☆ Buy extra ice
☆ Collect drinks and glasses
☆ Clear room
☆ Put out drinks
☆ Put out glasses – allow time for washing them if they are hired
☆ Distribute several ashtrays around the room.

SERVING A BUFFET

Arrange the food to show it off to best advantage. The dishes should be laid in the correct order for people to help themselves as they work along the table.

Have plates, together with knives and forks wrapped in napkins, at the start. Put sauces and dressings beside the dish that they go with. For about fifty people or more, it is best to have two supplies of plates and cutlery, and two of each dish, laid out at opposite ends, or on opposite sides, of the table.

If you cannot fit all the food on one table, the desserts could go on a side table until needed.

The tables of food and drink should not be positioned in a corner of the room, as this will cause a lot of congestion when people help themselves. They should be in the middle of a long wall so that there is lots of room. If you have the space, a table in the middle of the room is best of all.

LUNCH OR DINNER PARTY

These are more staightforward than a drinks or buffet party in that you will be catering for a small number of people. As before, plan the menu well ahead and do as much of the cooking in advance as possible. Or serve a straightforward main course such as a good joint of meat, with a soup or cold first course that can be prepared ahead, and cold desserts.

TEENAGE PARTIES

For a teenage party, the planning and preparations are the same as for a buffet (see above). The food should be simple and interesting, but not too unusual. In addition to the usual soft drinks, you could make up a non-alcoholic fruit punch, or for older teenagers a wine or cider cup.

You will also need to set up a music system in a safe place where people cannot bang into it, and to make up or buy tapes of party music.

CHILDREN'S PARTIES

Send out the invitations in plenty of time, and be quite clear about what time the party starts and ends.

The food should be fun but straightforward, and there should be a good mixture of savoury and sweet dishes.

You will need to plan the games in advance, and gather together all the things that will be needed. Have a mixture of games for individuals, pairs and teams.

You may want to organize a visit from Father Christmas. Father Christmas outfits can be hired from party shops. Otherwise you will need to plan an improvised outfit complete with hat and beard, and a large sack for the presents.

You will need to buy and wrap up prizes and/or presents for the guests.

Empty the room to be used as far as possible, and cover the carpet around the table where the food is to be served.

Chapter 6

DECORATIONS

You may want to choose a particular style for the decorations, such as traditional, modern, Victorian, Scandinavian and so on. Or you may want to choose a colour scheme. However, the most important point is to have fun with the decorations, and be ready to accept help and contributions from other members of the family – however young.

THE TREE

If you are buying a real tree you have a choice of two types: those with a clean-cut stem, which you throw away after Christmas; and those complete with their roots, which you can plant in the garden. The traditional tree with its sharp little needles has now been joined by other types of fir tree that make less mess. They are more expensive, but you may feel it is money well spent. To be sure of getting the size of tree you want, you can order one in advance from suppliers such as greengrocers and garden centres. You should do this in early December.

If you do not want a real tree, there is a wide variety of artificial ones on the market, ranging from those that look very realistic to highly decorative silver- and gold-coloured trees.

WHERE TO PUT THE TREE?

The first point to remember is that a tree that is going to be lit needs to be within easy reach of an electric socket, so that you can plug in the lights without having the flex trailing round the room. It needs to be in a place where people will not be brushing past it all the time, yet where it can be seen from as many directions as possible. Don't put the tree too near to a radiator or it will dry out prematurely.

CONTAINERS FOR THE TREE

Whatever type of tree you have, make sure that the container is large and heavy enough to match the size of tree. There must be no risk of the tree toppling over.

The best types of container are a bucket, a large enamel container such as a bread bin, or, if you have one big enough, a plant-pot holder.

If you have a fresh tree that you are going to replant in the garden later, you will need to put it in a container holding soil. If not, an easy and efficient way to fix the tree firmly in the container is with large pieces of brick or stone, wedging them in around the trunk so that it is held firmly upright.

If you are using something like a bucket, which is not very attractive, there are many ways to disguise it. If you are not keeping the tree afterwards, and it is therefore not going to be in soil that needs watering, or if you have an artificial tree that does not have its own container, you can decorate the container with coloured paper, or even wrap a generous piece of brown paper around it, and tie a wide, brightly coloured ribbon around with a big bow. If you will need to water the tree, cover the container with something that will not be affected if it gets wet – rush matting, flexible split-bamboo matting, a simple wooden box or a large round basket. Alternatively, you could just heap up pretend-presents around the container to hide it.

If you want to cover the soil of a planted tree, use cotton wool pulled out to look like snow, or spray on mock snow, or alternatively cover it with dried flowers, leaves or pot-pourri.

CHRISTMAS TREE LIGHTS

If you have a set of tree lights, get them out in good time. Lay them out on the ground and plug them in to test whether they are working. If they do not come on, check that each bulb is fully screwed in. If they still do not come on, you need to find out which bulb has gone by unscrewing each in turn and replacing it with a new one until they light up.

If you need to buy new lights, check that they meet the approved British safety standard. Buy a good make, and buy a set that is well packed in a sturdy box. This gives them better protection, and gives you something to store them in. Check the length of the flex, to make sure that it will reach the socket in the room where you are putting the tree. Check that the lights are well spaced so that they can be distributed all over the tree, and make sure that the lights and shades are securely fitted and well made.

DECORATIONS AROUND THE HOME

One of the most effective ways of decorating the house is to use lots of greenery from the garden together with other natural materials; this has the added advantage of being economical. A wide variety of decorations can be made from these materials, ranging from simple bowls and baskets of coloured cones, leaves and fruit to wreaths, garlands and table centres. Even arrangements of fresh flowers need not be too costly if they are filled out with sprays of evergreens. Begin in the autumn by collecting dried leaves and fir cones for painting, dried hydrangea heads to spray silver or gold, and any other interesting or unusual materials that you come across.

GOOD CONTAINERS FOR DECORATIONS

Baskets	Fill with cones and sprigs of fir; use sphagnum moss or Oasis to provide a firm base in the bottom of the basket if you want to include candles in the arrangement.
Bowls	Fill with dried leaves mixed with nuts, herbs and spices such as cinnamon sticks or sprays of rosemary, or pomanders made from oranges stuck with cloves.
Large jugs	Good for large sprays of dried flowers, greenery and fresh flower arrangements.

ITEMS THAT LOOK GOOD SPRAYED OR PAINTED

☆ hydrangea heads
☆ fir cones
☆ dried leaves
☆ fir
☆ holly and ivy
☆ lemons and tangerines
☆ bunches of walnuts and Brazil nuts
☆ red chilli peppers
☆ gourds

CHRISTMAS COLOUR COMBINATIONS

☆ Blue/green pine background with yellow/orange fruit
☆ Deep green with creamy white and yellow fresh flowers

☆ Red, green and gold
☆ Silver and blue

MAKING A WREATH

*Oasis ring or polystyrene foam ring, soaked; or raffia bound
    round a wire coathanger that has been pulled circular
    florist's wire for hanging*

*selection of evergreens — holly, ivy, cypress, spruce, juniper,
    pine, laurel; or herbs and spices — rosemary, bay, eucalyptus,
    sage*

ribbon, about 4 cm (1½ in) wide

*selection of nuts, cones, baubles, bunches of cinnamon sticks,
    tangerines and bunches of red chilli peppers for decorating*

Bind the florist's wire several times around the foam ring or raffia, and twist the ends together to form a loop from which to hang the wreath.

Wire any nuts and cones as illustrated; wire together bunches of chilli peppers by their stalks if used; if using tangerines, bend a piece of wire in half and push the ends through the tangerine.

Break the evergreens into small sprays and press stalks into the Oasis or foam ring, or bind onto raffia ring, to cover it. Distribute the decorations around the ring and attach with the wire.

Tie a bow in the ribbon and attach to the wreath. Alternatively you could tie a number of small bows.

MAKING A TABLE CENTRE

container – china dish or bowl, or basket
Oasis, cut to fit the container and soaked
selection of evergreens (see Making a Wreath, above)
baubles and other decorations (see Making a Wreath, above)
coloured ribbon
tall, thin candles – they can be of differing lengths

Line the container with a piece of plastic, such as a bin liner or a plastic bag cut to fit, and position the pieces of Oasis in it.

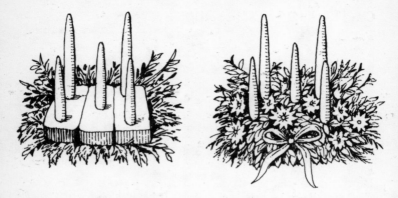

Cut short pieces of evergreens and stick them into the Oasis around the sides and at the corners of the arrangement. Position the candles in the Oasis, and then push in the rest of the greenery to cover it.

Add baubles and other decorations. Tie little bows in the ribbon and place in the foliage (or on the handles if there are any).

To make a decoration for a sideboard, or a window-sill, use a container to fit the space.

MAKING A GARLAND FOR A FIREPLACE OR BANISTER RAIL

piece of rope, or old tights, cut and/or tied to required length
selection of evergreens
selection of decorations } *See Making a Wreath*

Using the rope or tights as the base, bind on the evergreens to cover it completely, teasing some pieces out so that they trail. Distribute the decorations along the length of the garland and attach them.

CHECKLIST OF DECORATIONS

- holly
- mistletoe
- ivy
- evergreens for arrangements
- fir cones, nuts, leaves etc
- gold, silver and other paints
- fresh flowers and pot plants
- dried flowers
- candles
- containers

- Oasis
- tree
- tree lights
- tree decorations
- tinsel
- coloured baubles
- baby crackers
- coloured ribbon
- paper decorations – chains, streamers etc

THE TABLE

Christmas is the time to bring out the best cutlery, china, glass and table linen, and these alone will make the table look decorative. You could make an evergreen table centre, or use a bowl of fresh flowers. In each place setting you could have a little present, or a posy of dried flowers, or a little bunch of fabric flowers that have been dipped in porcelain fabric hardener and painted gold or whatever colour matches the rest of the table. Folded table napkins always look impressive and are easy to do. The water lily illustrated here sits on a place mat, while the tulip stands in a tumbler or wineglass. Candles, crackers and bowls of sweets, nuts, dates and figs complete the table.

CHECKLIST FOR THE TABLE

- glass and cutlery
- napkins, tablecloth, runner
- candles and candlesticks
- crackers

- sweet dishes
- table-centre decoration
- place setting decorations

Folding Napkins

Water lily

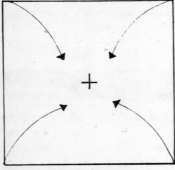

1 a. Lay the napkin out flat on a table and locate the centre.
  b. Fold each corner in to the centre.
  c. Work round again, folding each corner in to the centre.
  d. Repeat again.

3 a. Place a tumbler over the corners in the centre to pin them down and hold in place with your left hand.
  b. With your right hand feel underneath one of the corners for a free corner, and pull the point of the corner up to touch the side of the glass. Repeat with the corner next to it and so on with the first round of corners. Repeat with the next round of corners, and then with the final round.

2 a. Turn the folded napkin over.
  b. Fold each corner in to the centre.

4 Remove the tumbler from the centre. The napkin will now support itself.

Tulip

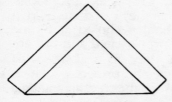

1 Lay the napkin out flat and fold corner B about three-quarters of the way up to corner A.

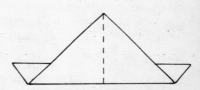

3 Turn the napkin over and, starting from the centre, concertina it together like a fan, with approximately 2 cm (¾ in) folds.

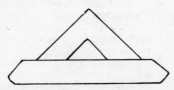

2 Fold up the lower, long edge of the napkin.

4 a. Take hold of the bottom end of the fan, and pull the side folds down and out.
   b. Separate the top corners a little to give a tulip shape.

THINGS FOR CHILDREN TO MAKE

Children love to join in making Christmas decorations, and there are plenty of things that they can do to help. It is also a good way to keep them occupied at a time when they are probably rather over-excited and you are very busy. If you feel that you need to organize what they do, you can give them specific projects, such as making the hanging decorations for the tree, arranging a table-centre decoration with greenery, candles and baubles, or making a Father Christmas mobile. Alternatively, you could turn it into a game, for example by organizing a competition to see who can make the longest paper chain. If the children want to put up decorations around the house, or decorate the tree themselves, give them a free hand. You can always make adjustments after they have gone to bed.

☆ Paper chains – packets of ready-gummed strips of coloured paper can be bought.
☆ Strings of Christmas cards.
☆ Cut-out stars, snowmen, Father Christmas, Christmas trees, angels, and plum puddings for the tree, made from coloured card, or from plain or corrugated card painted gold or silver, with a loop of gold or silver thread at the top to hang them from. (The shapes can be traced from pictures on cards or in magazines).
☆ Strings of popcorn, nuts and fruit for the tree.
☆ Play-dough decorations.
☆ Wreaths and discs of dried pasta shapes, popcorn, or leaves, glued to card, spray-painted gold and silver and decorated with ribbon bows.
☆ Christmas spheres made from pairs of wooden embroidery rings or wire coat-hangers, bound around with gold or silver tape, or greenery, and hung with coloured sweets or baubles. Painted and sprayed leaves, cones etc., to add to decorations.

Chapter 7

PRESENTS AND CARDS

LAST POSTING DATES

If you need to send cards and presents abroad, the first thing to do in the autumn is to check on the last posting dates, which for surface post to some of the further off or remoter parts of the world occur during September. The Post Office publishes leaflets listing the last posting dates for Christmas for both surface post and airmail.

PRESENTS

When it comes to shopping for presents there are two approaches. Either you can go out looking for inspiration, or you can plan what to get for each person, and where from, first. In practice, most people's shopping is probably a combination of both. However, it does save a lot of time and energy if you can plan what you want to get beforehand.

There is a third, very convenient, alternative: mail order. The usual mail order houses produce Christmas catalogues, as do most charities. In addition, high-quality foods such as cheeses, chocolates, smoked salmon, meats and so on, wines and other drinks, and items such as crafts and hobbies kits and equipment are available from specialist suppliers who advertise in newspapers and the relevant magazines. Keep an eye on the weekly and monthly women's magazines, as some have features on Christmas mail order catalogues. You choose the presents in the comfort of your own home, and they are delivered direct to the recipient. Begin organizing this in mid-November to make sure everything arrives in time.

For many people, however, having a good look round the shops is an important part of the build-up to Christmas. For those feeling lost for ideas, the following lists may help. If you are buying for someone with a particular interest or hobby, don't forget to try specialist shops or departments dealing in that activity as these can be a very fruitful source of gifts.

LUXURIES

make-up sets
herb sachets
boxes of soaps
pretty bottles for scent and hand
   lotions

hand-made stationery
pomanders
scented candles

FOLLOWERS OF FASHION

embroidered jacket
beaded or embroidered bag
hair decorations – combs, slides,
   bands etc

novelty watch or clock
novelty teapot

FOR THE HOME

planters
flower brick
candlesticks
lampshades
wicker baskets
photograph album
photograph frames

cushions
pot-pourri
dried flower or moss trees
tea cosy
tray
bridge set

FOR COOKS

nutmegs and grater
garlic pot

moulds for puddings etc
perspex cookery book stand
Kilner jars

FOR GARDENERS

terracotta pots
plant propagator
hose-reel winder

garden-tidy
gardening gloves
tool set for indoor gardeners

FOR HIM

waistcoat
leather belt
fashion braces

wine rack
fountain pen

PRESENTS TO MAKE

Presents that are home-made have an extra value because of the time and thought that has gone into them.

☆ Cooks can make chutneys and jams, sweets, biscuits, cakes, pâtés, bottled fruit, and fruit and herb vinegars.

☆ Flower arrangers can make dried flower arrangements and trees, and pot-pourri.

☆ Needleworkers can make embroidered handkerchiefs, hand towels and pillow cases, finger puppets for children, and all sorts of knitted clothes and toys.

WRAPPING PRESENTS

Presents should look as neat and attractive as possible, but this can be difficult to achieve when they are also an awkward shape.

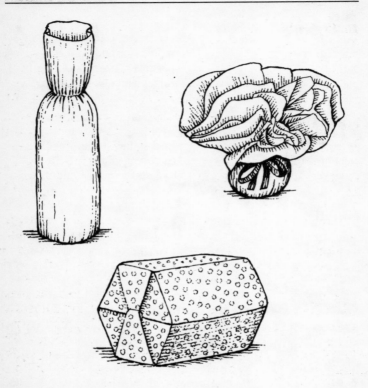

Round and multi-sided containers

Cut the paper to the right size. Lay it flat, right side down, and place the container on the paper on its side. Wrap the paper around the container and fix with double-sided tape.

At one end, fold the paper over the end in small sections. If the container has sides, the sections should match them. Do this by folding over one section, then the sections on either side of it, then those on either side of them, and so on all the way round and stick down in the centre. Repeat at the other end.

Ball-shaped objects

Take two square pieces of paper of the same size. Place one on top of the other so that the corners do not match up. It looks effective if you use papers that are different colours, textures or finishes. Place the object in the centre. Gather up the paper by bringing together the four corners and bunching all the paper together on top of the object. Grip firmly and fix with sticky tape. Cover this with a ribbon tied in a bow. Separate out the layers of paper. You can use pinking shears to trim the edges of the paper to finish off.

Bottles

Cut the paper to size. Lay the paper flat, right side down, and then lay the bottle on its side on the paper. At the bottom end, fold in the paper and stick down as for a circular object (above). Stand the bottle up.

Then you can cut some card and roll it to make a cylinder of the same diameter as the bottle. Put this over the neck to extend the bottle shape, and treat the top end like the bottom end. Alternatively bring the two sides of the paper together against the neck of the bottle, folding the excess into a pleat on either side. Fold the top of the paper down a couple of times and stick it down against the neck of the bottle.

Squashy objects

Items such as jumpers can be very awkward to wrap. Cut two pieces of card just bigger than the item, and sandwich it between them before wrapping.

Containers for edible presents

If you are making edible presents such as bottled fruits, biscuits or sweets, begin collecting containers for them in good time.

☆ Glass jars and bottles: can be decorated by painting on patterns or flowers.

☆ Baskets, covered boxes: for sweets and biscuits.

Make sure that they are well labelled, and have storage instructions written on them.

Line boxes and baskets with waxed paper, foil or cellophane to prevent any contents leaking and spoiling the container.

Covering a box

FOR THE BASE OF THE BOX:
Measure the width of the box (measurement A). Measure the depth of the box (measurement B). Add together the width of the box, plus twice the depth of the box on each side (i.e. the depth × 4), plus an extra 1 cm (⅜ in) on each side. Calculate the length in the same way. Cut the paper to these dimensions.

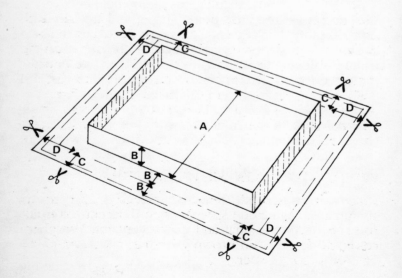

Place the paper right side down on a firm surface and lightly mark out the dimensions above on the wrong side to give you the exact position of the box on the paper. Draw in line C at each corner and cut along it.

Place the box in position on the paper. Fold the paper over the two long sides, tuck into the bottom of the box and stick down. Cut off the excess paper at each corner by cutting along line D. Fold the paper over the two short sides, tuck down inside the box and stick down.

Repeat for the lid.

TAGS, CARDS AND WRAPPING PAPER

This is another activity that the children will enjoy.

TO MAKE CARDS AND TAGS

Use pieces of plain coloured paper, cut to size and decorated with coloured stars, or patterns and shapes drawn or painted on. Cut down used Christmas cards, using either the front of the card only, or the double thickness. Or you could scallop the edges for a tag.

Punch a hole in the top left-hand corner. Thread a doubled-over piece of ribbon through the hole, then pass the ends of the ribbon through the loop and pull tight.

PRINTING YOUR OWN WRAPPING PAPER

Paper can be printed, stencilled, spattered, sprayed or sponged (use a natural sponge) with different-coloured paints to create original and exciting effects. Use plain coloured paper, plain brown wrapping paper, or white or cream lining paper.

CHECKLIST FOR PRESENTS AND CARDS

- check posting dates
- cards
- stamps
- wrapping paper
- tags

- ribbon
- bows
- decorative bags and boxes
- double-sided tape

Chapter 8

MASTER PLAN

A day-by-day plan for the last month before Christmas will enable you to bring together all the different aspects of preparations, and should ensure that nothing gets overlooked. Events and activities that other members of the family are involved in should also be incorporated. The following should all be included in the plan, if relevant to you.

Order turkey
tree
drinks
hire glasses

Check last date for posting parcels
posting cards

Check times of carol services
school events
buses and trains over the holiday
local shop opening times over the holiday

Test tree lights
Check/replace decorations

Check prescription supplies
Make appointment at hairdresser

MASTER PLAN

NOVEMBER 28	29	30	DECEMBER 1	2	3	4
Order turkey	Cooking day	Send out invitations	Book hairdresser Order drinks and glasses for party	Order tree	Check tree lights and decorations	Check last posting dates – parcels
5	6	7	8	9	10	11
Check prescriptions	Christmas shopping day Meet friend for lunch	Check carol service times	Write cards	Free day	Wrap presents	Last chance to make the cake

12	**13**	**14**	**15**	**16**	**17**	**18**
Check bus and train times	Cooking day	Dry cleaning and mending	Check last posting dates – first and second class	Re-stock drinks cabinet	Last big shop	All presents wrapped

19	**20**	**21**	**22**	**23**	**24**	**25**
Marzipan cake Make mince pies	Collect tree Children to party	Make up guest beds Decorate tree and house	Defrost turkey (depending on size)	Ice cake Collect drinks Last-minute shopping	Fill car with petrol Start Xmas dinner Collect turkey (if fresh)	

Mending
Dry cleaning
Prepare rooms for house guests

Last big shop
Replenish drinks cabinet
All presents wrapped
Decorate tree and house

Last-minute shopping
Collect drinks
Collect turkey
Fill car with petrol
Defrost food

When planning all the Christmas activities, remember to build in some time for relaxing, to meet friends for lunch, or just to put your feet up for an hour.

Chapter 9

EMERGENCIES OVER CHRISTMAS

PLUMBING

FROZEN PIPES

To find out which pipe is frozen, turn each tap on in turn to see which one is not running. If the pipe is accessible, first turn the tap on and then apply heat to the pipe near the tap – it will travel along the pipe to the frozen part – or apply heat near another outlet so that the melting ice can escape. Bind a cloth around the pipe and apply heat – either from a hair-drier or blow-heater, or use a hot-water bottle or hot water from a kettle. If a drainpipe or WC cistern has frozen, pour salt into them.

BURST PIPES

Turn off the water coming from the cold tank. If this is not possible, tie up the stopcock on the tank so that it does not refill. Then drain down the system by turning on all the taps. If you turn off the water supply to the boiler or central heating system, switch off the boiler until the water supply is restored.

If electric wires or cables are nearby, turn off the electricity at the mains.

First aid repairs can be done to pipes by rubbing soap

into the split and binding a rag around it; by tying it up with a rag saturated in paint; alternatively use epoxy resin and a glass fibre bandage, following the manufacturer's instructions.

These are only temporary repairs and will need watching carefully. The water supply should be restored very gently and at low pressure.

ELECTRICAL REPAIRS

Be careful not to overload the electrical system by having too many appliances working at once or several items plugged into an adaptor running off the same socket.

BLOWN FUSES

If the problem affects only one appliance, either the fuse in the plug has blown, or the flex is faulty. Check the flex – if it is hot, frayed or damaged in any way, it will need to be replaced by an electrician. If the flex is all right, put a new fuse in the plug. If the fault is in several appliances, or in a section of the house, a main fuse has blown in the fuse box. Repair this if you know how, or wait until an electrician can call.

POWER CUTS

If all the electricity in the house and in neighbouring houses goes off, there is a power cut. Turn off all electric fires, blankets, cooker rings, kettles and irons, as you may have forgotten about them by the time the electricity comes on again.

☆ Keep the refrigerator and freezer closed.

☆ If you use candles, put them all in proper candle-holders, and do not position them near curtains, near the tree or any other decorations, or anywhere where they could catch a draught. Do not leave them alight in an empty room.

STAINS

CHOCOLATE

☆ On clothes – scrape off the excess, and soak the garment in a pre-wash soaking product, or lukewarm water and biological washing powder. If it will not come out, soak in borax solution.
☆ On furnishings – sponge with warm water.

GLUE

☆ Water-soluble glue should come out with normal washing.
☆ Waterproof or insoluble glue should be treated with acetone, white spirit or lighter fuel.

GRAVY/BLOOD

☆ Soak in a cold solution of a pre-soak product or biological washing powder. Then wash as normal.

WAX

☆ Place blotting paper over the wax marks and iron with a hot iron.

WHITE WINE/BEER

☆ If washable, wash at a high temperature. Otherwise treat with one part white vinegar to four parts water, and rinse thoroughly.

RED WINE

☆ Mop up the excess, and then sprinkle with salt. Sponge with warm water and immediately rinse off with cold water.

☆ On carpets and upholstery, sprinkle with salt and rinse with warm water.

ILLNESS

INDIGESTION AND UPSET STOMACH

To reduce your chances of suffering from indigestion or an upset stomach, take plenty of time when you are eating a large meal, and do not drink alcohol on an empty stomach. Indigestion and queasiness are both made worse by fizzy drinks, so if you begin to suffer from either, drink cold, still water. If you are suffering from indigestion, antacid pills may help.

HANGOVER

You can reduce the risk of getting a hangover, without spoiling your fun, by not mixing different types of alcoholic drinks, by alternating alcoholic and non-alcoholic drinks, and by drinking plenty of water. If you have a hangover, do not take aspirins, or any pills containing aspirin, as they irritate the stomach; paracetamol is better. Drink plenty of still water or milk; hot, sweet tea is a good reviver.

Remember to stock up the medicine chest before Christmas with:
   antiseptic lotion and cream
   cotton wool
   indigestion pills or powders
   painkillers
   plasters

INDEX

Bold page numbers refer to recipes

THE FAMILY MATTERS SERIES